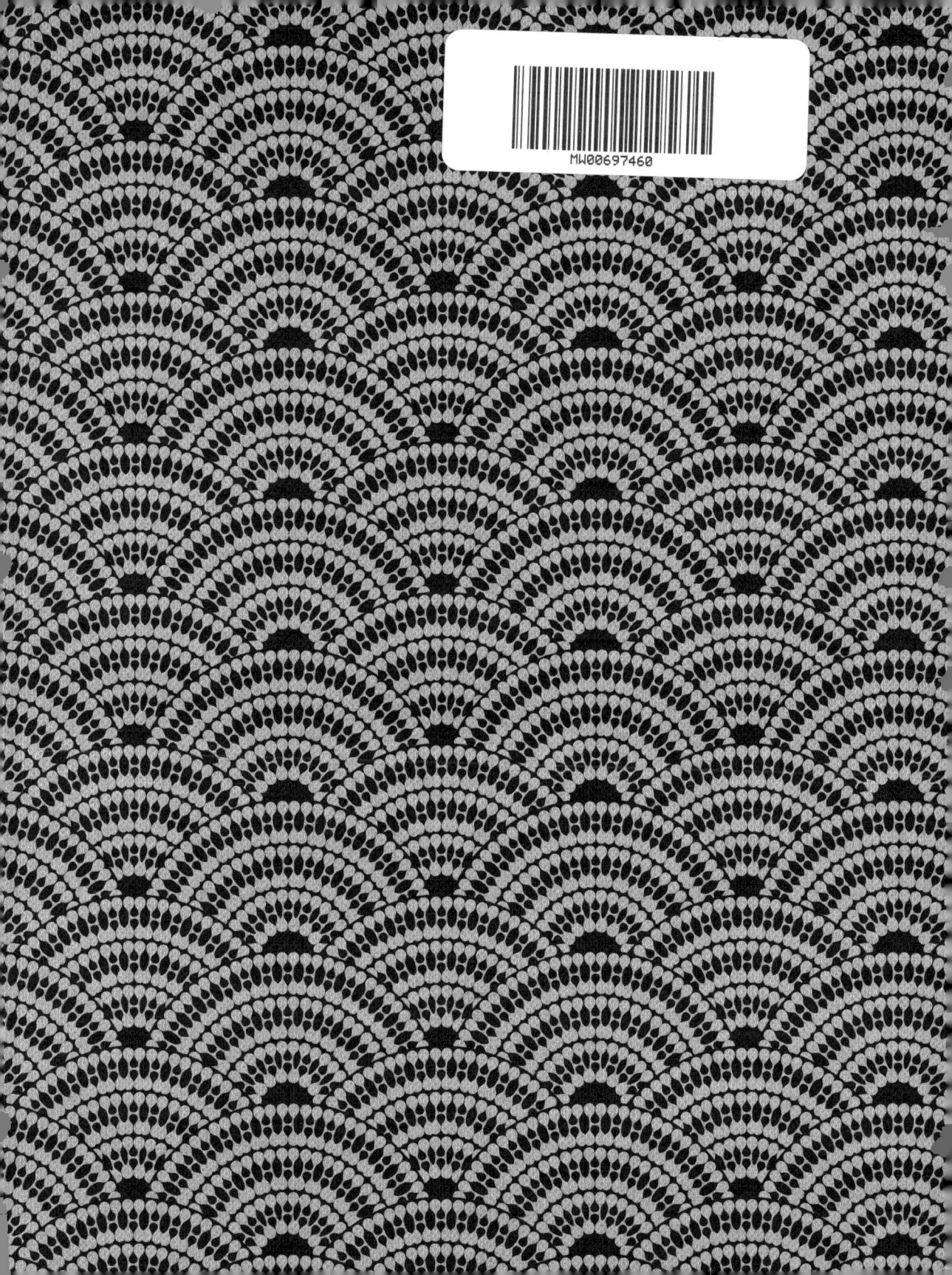

House Industries

YORKLYN, DELAWARE, U.S.A.

House Industries

In 1993, we started a design company that existed only on paper, but those sketches, scribbles and thoughts provided the fuel that made House Industries a reality. We reimagined the alphabet and made some fonts, which eventually drew us into everything from clothing and furniture to ceramics and space travel. Despite the unlikely mix of media that House Industries became, we never found a better way to realize ideas than by putting pencil to paper. But this journal isn't about our work, it's about yours. Whether they're sublime, stupid, monumental or mundane, your drawings, doodles, personal reflections and passing fancies have potential to become something inspiring.

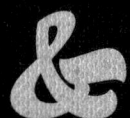

ISBN-978-0-451-49871-7

PUBLISHED IN THE U.S.A. BY CLARKSON POTTER/PUBLISHERS, AN IMPRINT OF
THE CROWN PUBLISHING GROUP, A DIVISION OF PENGUIN RANDOM HOUSE LLC, NEW YORK.
CLARKSON POTTER IS A TRADEMARK AND POTTER WITH COLOPHON IS
A REGISTERED TRADEMARK OF PENGUIN RANDOM HOUSE LLC.
CROWNPUBLISHING.COM • CLARKSONPOTTER.COM

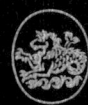

CLARKSON POTTER/PUBLISHERS
NEW YORK